Preface 5
Parents' Guide 5
Preliminary Groundwork 7
Using the Workbook 9
Why Aren't the Dinosaurs in the Creation Story? 9
Introduction 10
Making Sense of The Creation Account 17
Two Very Different "Creation" Accounts 25
Adam and Eve 30
The Fulfillment 34
When Things Make Sense 36
In Conclusion ....

Preface

I took Physical Science my freshman year in college. It was an 8:00 a.m. class. The professor shuffled into the classroom holding an opened umbrella. He had this unkempt look about him, like he had slept in his clothes. He stood there with the opened umbrella over his head and spoke to us about never expecting the expected when trying to put the world together.

The first day we worked out word problems. Given certain information, you had to set up an equation and then solve it. As he worked them through on the board, they seemed so simple and easy. He warned us not to be fooled, and gave us a set of problems to work out every night on our own before we would do them in class the next day. But who "had time" to work out a problem that sounded that easy?

The following Monday morning he gave us a test. As I tried to work out the problems, panic set in. There had to be something missing. It seemed so simple when he did it, and now, try as I might, it just wouldn't work. Only when forced to work out the problem ourselves did I discover that I couldn't tell what I knew from what he knew. Unless I was willing to own it, it would never belong to me.

Now, when I am asked biblical questions, I usually refrain from simply giving the answers. Instead, I look for ways the kids can process how they see and understand the Scriptures. Only by "owning it" *before* the solution is presented, does it belong to them. Besides being effective, it is much more interesting, enjoyable, and most of all, unforgettable.

Sometimes, both as parents and/or teachers, we don't know what it is we don't know until that defining moment when our children turn to us with all the confidence in the world. Then we suddenly realize that the questions they are asking require answers totally different from the ones we grew up with. And we are facing the startling discovery that our children's faith experience is not going to be exactly the same as ours.

Why Aren't the Dinosaurs in the Creation Story? is the first in a series of family Scripture studies in Liguori's "Lighthouse Series" that has developed over years of teaching families with young people, and of being asked questions that somehow fall between the cracks of the *Catechism of the Catholic Church* and the theologians. They are the questions from the next generation.

That being the case, it makes sense first to work out our own questions of faith before we begin to try to answer the questions from the next generation. This family Scripture study is a sequel to a "mother" book that takes us on a faith journey—from our parents' Church...to our Church...and then beyond into our children's Church. The title is *Keepers of the Light.* Using lighthouse stories and analogies, it parallels the role of the lighthouse keeper to the keeper of the light of faith in the family, thereby revealing insights of how both roles have had to change over the years. *Keepers of the Light* points to a challenge all parents face: how to answer the questions of the next generation. The family Scripture study is the next step in that process.

While each of the family Scripture studies can stand on its own, the full experience of really "owning" the whole process of passing on the light of faith will only be made complete by combining these Scripture studies with the *Keepers of the Light.* It is our hope that the Lighthouse Series will help you and your family "keep the light" of faith burning.

Parents' Guide

Before we can help our children move forward in the faith process, we need to put our own faith experience into perspective. Each Scripture study, therefore, seeks first to bridge the gap between the generations. By using specific stories from *Keepers of the Light,* you will be able to reevaluate for yourself what you thought you knew before being drawn into today's Church. Stories stir our memories and open our hearts to realize how important our Catholic experience of Church truly is.

Preliminary Groundwork

Theme: To rekindle memories of your own childhood faith experience.

Purpose: To put three generations of faith experiences into perspective.

Goal: To create a defining moment wherein you as a parent will arrive at the conclusion that you must reinvest in your own religious education to be better prepared to answer the difficult questions your children will inevitably ask.

Materials Needed:

- *Keepers of the Light,* Phyllis Calvey, Liguori Lifespan, © 2000 (ID# 55430) $9.95
- a copy of *Why Aren't the Dinosaurs in the Creation Story?* for each person in your family or group
- Bibles, one for each person
- pens or pencils

Begin by:

1. Reading "What Goes Around, Comes Around," on page 43 in *Keepers of the Light.*
2. Turn to *Why Aren't the Dinosaurs in the Creation Story?*
3. Jot down your reflections on the following questions:
   A. What are some of your favorite childhood memories of Church?

B. Note three specific changes that have taken place in the Church since you were a child (Latin Mass, fasting for hours before communion, etc.).

C. What were your religious questions like back then? Did they get answered?

Follow through with:

1. Read the preface to *Keepers of the Light,* omitting the last four paragraphs.
2. Answer the following questions:
   A. Write down some of the questions your children have asked about religion.

B. Are they different or the same as the questions you posed growing up? Explain.

____

____

____

____

C. Do you feel comfortable answering the questions your children ask? Why or why not?

____

____

____

____

Using the Workbook

It is important to familiarize yourself with the whole booklet before you "study" it with anyone else. This will help you "retell" the content of the book—rather than reading it—to your children.

The bolded sections are the "hands-on" parts of the study. As you come to each one, give everyone the time needed to answer the questions. It is important to ask everyone to share his or her own answers/reflections/experiences before you read the responses given in the text.

In the section, "Two Very Different 'Creation' Accounts," ask everyone to open the Bible, fill in the blanks, and answer the questions concerning the seven days of creation. As you go through the meaning of the seven days, discuss each day separately. Read aloud "day one" from the Bible. Then give everyone a chance to share answers and reflections. Close treatment of this day by reading the teaching for the day. Beside "day one" have them jot down the concept. Then read aloud "day two," etc.

In the section, "The Fulfillment," all are asked to write the most obvious match for Moses, the first Covenant, Adam, sin, etc. Following this exercise, you might find it helpful to have 1 Corinthians 15:45-47 and Romans 5:12-21 read aloud. These readings from Paul are wonderful explanations of Jesus as the last Adam.

If you are leading a larger group, continue with this format until the last three questions on pages 36-37. At that point, have people break up into smaller discussion groups. Designate a person from each group to take notes and later share the group's reflections. After the small group discussion, return again to the larger group to have each group share with the larger group.

Why Aren't the Dinosaurs in the Creation Story?

Introduction

Many of us have difficulties telling our children that "Adam and Eve" is a story, simply because we have never really "worked out the problem" for ourselves. The Church acknowledges parents as the first and foremost educators of their children, so we need a basic knowledge of the Church's traditions, sacraments, and teachings on morality, peace, and justice.

Basic to all these teachings is the Bible. Some of the desire to know the Bible may be prompted by a sense of inadequacy when approached by fundamentalist Christians. Certainly, the millennium brought religion to the forefront in many diverse aspects. However, our deepest need to know the Bible comes from being parents of a new generation of Internet children who insist on answers to the difficult questions of faith, biblical questions that were never dealt with in our time, because, ironically, Catholics were greatly discouraged from reading the Bible.

Recently, our pastor presented a basic overview of the Bible. Most of the presentation was geared toward encouraging families to feel comfortable about reading the Scriptures. It reinforced the teaching that the Bible is not to be taken literally. *The Good News Bible, Catholic Study Edition* (American Bible Society, New York, 1979), clearly explains that different kinds of literary forms were used to teach a religious truth. For example, it states that "the first eleven chapters of Genesis are much closer to mythical forms of writing," and that "a myth is a profoundly true statement which speaks to universal aspects of life and reality...whose meaning rises above time and space" (page xi).

Through a hands-on approach to learning, we have a chance to find the "missing pieces." Process is the key to "owning it." Through the process of this family study, it becomes clear why the biblical writers chose "story" as the way to teach religion, for the inspired biblical story "gifts" even the most hesitant person into a "conversation" with the divine. This "dialog" helps us, in turn, to sort out our own questions of faith, whereby we are enabled to better answer the questions our children now have.

Making Sense of the Creation Account

I remember when Rita, our youth minister, approached Brian and me to ask if we'd be interested in teaching one of the courses for a new miniseries she was offering for the ninth grade. What I specifically remember is how my knees began to shake at the mere thought of teaching ninth-graders. Rita went on to assure us that everything we needed would be in the teacher's guide that came with the program. Well, that being the case, we agreed. Since Brian and I had participated in Bible study for many years, she decided to give us the module that dealt with the creation story.

The first step was to read the teacher's guide with all the background explanations, and then go through the workbook itself and answer all the questions. The assignment was to look up and read the first chapter of Genesis, and then to answer the questions in the workbook. For example, "God created the world in ______ days. What was created on the third day? God created the sun, moon, and stars on the ______ day?" And I thought, hmm, Rita was right. This was not going to be so difficult after all.

We came in feeling very prepared to guide the students through a carefully designed course. After the usual introductions and icebreakers, I directed them to turn to the first page of their workbooks. Before I even had a chance to tell them to read the first chapter of Genesis, a hand went up. "You have a question already?" I asked smiling.

Don't people always begin in this way when they have the most profound question to ask? "I know this is a stupid question," he began, "but I always wanted to know why the dinosaurs weren't in the creation story?" I suddenly noticed that all the kids were looking down at their workbook, and only at that moment did I realize the illustrations that were chosen to go with the story of creation. There, spread across the two pages, were a giant brontosaurus, a stegosaurus, and a pterodactyl!

Now all the students were looking to us for an answer. My first instinct was to immediately revert back to the teacher's guide Rita promised would have all the answers we'd need. I made a quick mental check. Not one mention of dinosaurs. There was no way we were prepared to answer the question the way it needed to be answered. But here were expectant kids, and we knew we had to take their Bible questions seriously. Truly, this was one question that was not going to go away; being extinct, just think how popular dinosaurs are. For example, when we were kids—think back for a moment—who was the most famous little cartoon dinosaur?

Dino, of course. We all remember lovable little Dino from the Flintstones™. Our son, Trevor, took dinosaurs very seriously. When he was little, he had a "Land of the Lost" cave set that included many different kinds of dinosaurs, and he took great pride in knowing all their names. Who would qualify as the most famous dinosaur for this younger generation?

Anyone with small children has heard of big, purple Barney and can most likely even sing the famous Barney song. Dinosaurs are on cereal boxes, vitamins, and fruit snacks. And after the film *Jurassic Park,* it's safe to say the focus on dinosaurs is here to stay. A good answer was definitely needed for this question.

The best way to do this is to realize the importance of providing a time and place for people to "put" the stories of the Bible.

Our minds have a sort of filing system. When we hear something, our mind immediately seeks to file it somewhere. For example, read the following three words/names (out loud). As you read/hear each one, write down in the space provided what immediately comes to mind, what events are associated with the word, and what specific date in history you connect it with. Ready?

Please fill in the blanks:

"Abraham Lincoln"
What comes to mind? ________________________

What events? ________________________

What date in history? ________________________

"The Pilgrims"
What comes to mind? ________________________

What events? ________________________

What date in history? ________________________

"Creation"
What comes to mind? ________________________

What events? ______________________________

What date in history? ______________________________

Some of the words associated with Abraham Lincoln are, "Honest Abe," a top hat and beard, and the abolitionist president. Events were the Civil War, The Proclamation of Emancipation, and the time was the 1860's. When people hear the word Abraham Lincoln, their minds associate it with a picture, a specific time and place to file it, and an idea of the events surrounding Abraham Lincoln that gives a feeling of justice and pride.

People easily associate the word "Pilgrims" with the Mayflower, Thanksgiving, Massachusetts, and the year 1620. Again, a single word brings to mind a familiar time and event.

But the word creation usually meets with a completely different reaction. When we did that same exercise with our ninth-graders, I remember asking Chris to share with the class what he thought of when I said the word "creation." All of a sudden, he got this blank look on his face, and for a moment I thought I could see this one-celled ameba pass across his eyes. Then, he threw his head back and said: "You know, it's just too much to think about." I thought that was a good answer for someone trying to think back to the very beginning of time!

In our plan to answer the question, we decided to start with a time line that would first give a concrete look at how scientists would estimate the physical creation of the earth and what developed next.

Fill in the following time line. From left to right, list and date these five events in the following order. After you finish the time line, note the language and the events recorded, and fill in the blank.

1. How old is the earth? ______________________________

2. When did dinosaurs live? ______________________________

3. When did dinosaurs become extinct? ______________________________

4. When did Homo sapiens "of modern appearance" first show up on earth?

____

5. What is the date of the oldest known human site found in North America?

____

First time line:

1. 2. 3. 4. 5.

The creation of ______________________________

I'd like to share some of the answers people had to the question, "How old would you say the earth is?" People guessed between one, two, and three billion years. Quite a few said they had absolutely no idea.

Actually, well into the late nineteenth century some scientists still believed the earth to be only hundreds of millions of years old. All the scientific information I am going to present comes from National Geographic™. The following is from an article in the January 1998 issue. "On a remote road cut in Western Australia, in layers of sediment deposited 2.6 billion years ago, geologist Bruce Simonson found tiny beadlike grains of glass—evidence, he believes, of a colossal meteorite impact. By comparing them with spherules collected on other continents, he hopes to reconstruct what our planet looked like back in the 'good old days'—when one-celled organisms ruled the earth."

In another article, from March of 1998, a tiny ball of carbon nestled in a cavity was etched from a rock on what is now an island off Greenland; it is said to be 3.86 billion years old. The article went on to say it may be the oldest evidence of life on earth. Sometimes I wonder how they come up with the .86 billion. And still there are conjectures that "some 4.6 billion years ago, a cloud of dust condensed into planet earth, which soon turned molten from meteorite impacts and radioactive decay."

But for our time line, let's use 3.86 billion years for what scientists estimate to be the oldest evidence of life on earth. When would you say the dinosaurs fit into this time line? People guessed from one hundred and twenty million years ago to five hundred million. Again, according to National Geographic™, there were many periods of dinosaurs. But since our children are most familiar with the Jurassic period, let's use that date. The Jurassic period began 208 million years ago, followed by their extinction approximately 65 million years ago.

Let's take a look at when humans come into the picture. When did humans walk the earth? Homo sapiens of modern appearance displayed human traits and behaviors such as big game hunting, complex tool technology, and the first good evidence of artistic symbols. This was the biggest gap. People guessed anywhere from twelve thousand to one million years ago.

Most scientific evidence concurs that Homo sapiens of modern appearance showed up around 125,000 years ago, with the earliest evidence coming from Africa. Around 14,000 years ago, and possibly earlier, humans moved into North America. The oldest known human site in North America was discovered in Meadowcroft, Pennsylvania and goes back to between 14,000 and 12,000 B.C.E.

Look closely at the time line, the language, the events recorded. This is a time line with a clear purpose. It is a scientific attempt to reconstruct the beginnings of the physical creation of the earth, follow what developed next, and see where humankind fits into the picture. It is a time line showing the time and event of the infancy of the earth and its development from that point on. Perhaps we could label it *"The Creation of the Earth."*

Now let's build an entirely different time line.

From left to right, list and date these events in the following order. After you finish the time line, note the language and the events recorded, and fill in the blank.

1. The date most scholars agree the creation story in Genesis dates back to.

____

2. **The date most scholars agree the story of Abraham and Sarah dates back to.**

____

3. **The date the Pentateuch, the first five books of the Bible, were written.**

____

4. **When did David reign?**

____

5. **The period the prophets wrote.**

____

6. **The birth of Jesus.**

____

Second time line:

1. 2. 3. 4. 5. 6.

The creation of ________________________

The second time line was much more difficult for people—it's just not something most of us stop to think about. Traditionally, Moses is credited with writing the Pentateuch, the first five books of the Bible. He lived somewhere between 1300 and 1200 B.C.E. Actually, they were written later—by several authors over several generations—but the events described go much further back. For example, the story of Abraham and Sarah has been dated to around 1900 B.C.E. The origin of the story of creation in Genesis dates back even further, to about 2500 B.C.E. If we take the time line forward, we find David around the year 1000, the various prophets between 850 and 450 B.C.E. Finally, the event of the birth of Jesus was so epochal that we Christians later marked time based on it. Let us compare the two time lines by taking a closer look at the specific language used in each, and the intent of purpose.

Again, it's plain to see the first time line is obviously dealing with the scientific view of the physical creation of the earth. But take a close look at the second time line. Notice how different the language is. There seems to be no interest in recreating the earth at its infancy. Certainly, the dinosaur period had long come and gone. Humankind had inhabited the earth for thousands of years. There was a long period of time between the written word and the beginning of time itself. It seems something very different is being talked about in the creation account. Most of our people said the first graph definitely described the physical creation of the earth, and many guessed the second graph was describing the creation of religious awareness.

To be more precise, the Book of Genesis records the beginnings of Israel and its religion emerging in the midst of a world already full of religions dedicated to worshiping a variety of idols. Genesis is the account of the creation of the Hebrew religion. The Bible never concerns itself with explaining a scientific time line of the infancy of the earth. Nor would it have a need to mention an animal that became extinct sixty-five million years before the creation account was written. Dinosaurs came and went long before humankind. The Bible is a religious book that deals with religious matters, and therefore more concerned with the beginning of hearing God's word than with the beginning of time. And when we fill in the time line to read, *"The Creation of the Hebrew Religion,"* it suddenly all begins to make sense.

First time line:

1.
2.
3.
4.
5.
6.

The creation of ______________________________

Second time line:

1.
2.
3.
4.
5.
6.

The creation of ______________________________

Two Very Different "Creation" Accounts

We're going to look at two very different "creation" accounts.

In this exercise, draw a line down the middle of the space provided. At the top of the left column write "Scientific Description of the Beginning of the World." List what language you think scientists would use to describe how the earth was "created." List seven words or phrases people associate with a scientific account of attempting to describe the beginnings of the earth.

At the top of the right column write "The Biblical Description of the Days of Creation." List in order what was created on each of the seven "days." Compare the two accounts, and see if they seem to you to be describing something very different.

How did you do? How did the language of the two different creation accounts compare? Did the account given in the Bible seem like a literal description of the creation of the world?

The phrase people most commonly associate with a scientific account of describing the earth being formed in the beginning is "The Big Bang." Other answers people write are, "fire," "meteorite impacts," "chemical reaction," "energy," "volcanic activity," and "cloud of dust."

While people generally know enough to state what God created on the first and the seventh day, most get confused over the order of the rest. I would like to spend some time examining the days of creation in more detail, since, if it isn't a literal account of the world being created, we need to understand what is described, and why a six-day framework was chosen. Rather than listing the days of creation, I think it would be more effective if we looked at the precise words used in the Genesis account.

Open your Bibles and read the first chapter of Genesis as well as verses 1 through 4 of Chapter Two. After reading the descriptions of each day, fill in the blanks and answer the following questions.

1. ______________________________ was created on the first day.

2. The ______________________________ were created on the second day.

3. ______________________________ was created on the third day.

What is the firmament described in day two?

____

Between the second and third day, the waters were separated twice.

On the second day, how are the waters separated?

____

On the third day, how are the waters separated?

____

4. ______________________ was created on the fourth day.

5. ______________________ was created on the fifth day.

6. ______________________ was created on the sixth day.

7. On the seventh day God ______________________.

Everyone finished?

When I was young, I remember reading the days of creation and never once batting an eye. But when we covered the days of creation with our ninth-graders, we got quite a different reaction. Let's look at each of the days separately, and see how spiritual concepts are developed with the idea of each day.

According to Genesis, light is created on the first day. Listen to those beautiful words, "Then God said, 'Let there be light'; and there was light. And God saw that the light was good" (1:3-4a). When we read the first day of creation, Terry slapped his forehead and said: "I'm really starting to get this. We just read how in the beginning the world was in darkness, it was void and had no form. It was in darkness because the people didn't know who God was. I mean, we say it all the time: 'The light just went on!' And, symbolically, it came on for those people because they finally understood who God was."

Now that's the difference between seeing the account as literal and understanding that something symbolic of religious significance is happening. At this point, the Hebrew religion had no form or shape. There was no plan, no rules, no commandments had yet been established. This is the story of how the Jewish faith saw its origins. It was written for people who were seeking God in a world that was void and without form until this time. For the person seeking scientific answers, it sheds no light.

The inspired author used concepts that were already familiar, like the six-day framework, to speak of spiritual realities showing the development of God's plan for humankind. Light is created on the first day. The first concept is that there is a living God. Picture a scene of humankind groping in darkness with pagan religions and idols. Remember that humankind had long since inhabited the earth, and had practiced many forms of idol worship. Suddenly, light came upon the earth through a people who was beginning to grasp the nature and reality of the living God. Later on in the scriptural tradition, we see that light is understood as wisdom: Without light, one cannot understand anything. After establishing the concept of the one living God, it follows that God must have separated light and darkness from each other, but they are both contained in the same day, depicting the presence of both good and evil. This biblical concept brings choice into the picture. (The second chapter of Genesis will name God the "LORD God" to distinguish God from all pagan gods. The story of the Hebrew Scriptures is about the relationship that develops between Israel and the one true God.)

On the second day the heavens are created. The second concept is that God dwells in heaven, humans live on earth. The *Catechism of the Catholic Church* says it beautifully:

> The Scriptural expression "heaven and earth" means all that exists, creation in its entirety. It also indicates the bond, deep within creation, that both unites heaven and earth and distinguishes the one from the other: "the earth" is the world of men, while "heaven" or "the heavens" can designate both the firmament and God's own "place" (CCC 326).

While there was no question the Israelites knew God is responsible for creating everything, the interest of the inspired author did not lie in defining the universe—that kind of language would fit under the column on the scientific description of the beginning of time. The inspired author wanted the people to understand the meaning of their own existence on earth in relation to "the heavens," which represents God's dwelling place—again, a spiritual concept, not physical or geographical.

On the third day, water, dry land, and plants appear. I'm a visual person, and it helps to have a picture in my mind to understand a concept. I must admit that the waters always confused me. In the beginning, water is everywhere: in the heavens, above the heavens, on earth...it covers everything. I used to skip over the firmament part. I had to force myself to go through the separation of the waters one step at a time. I only really got a clearer picture of what was happening when

I realized the waters were separated *twice*. The first separation was vertical, an up and down separation of the waters that were contained above the heavens and the waters on the earth itself. The firmament or expanse that separated the waters was heaven itself, which I could picture physically as the clouds in the sky that held the waters in place until God sent the spiritual heavenly waters to the earth. With this, it made sense that the first separation of the waters happened the second day when the heavens are defined.

Then, on the third day, another separation of the waters takes place, this time horizontal. The seas are now contained in one place, separated from the land. Another concept develops. The "seas" represent a dissolving in God, and the earth or dry land refers to humans being separated from God. If you notice, religion is often symbolized through the "seas" themselves. When the journey becomes impassable, Moses parts the "seas of religious confusion." When the prophet Jonah runs away from God, he is thrown into the "seas," where he is most intimately confronted with God's presence. The Book of Jeremiah talks about a time when the "fishers" will come. It is no coincidence that many of the apostles were fishermen. Only one person ever walks on the "sea"—Jesus. On the third day of creation, everything is provided for religion to "grow" in the life-giving waters.

On the fourth day, the sun, the moon, and the stars are created. Now, as soon as I wrote this down on the board in class, the kids immediately said, "Wow, the sun was created on the fourth day, but light was created on the first day." Did you have a similar reaction? Again, it is so easy to see it wasn't meant to be a literal account. I remember recently talking to a first grade teacher. She was laughing as she told me how she started writing the days in order on the board in class. She wrote down light, and only when she actually got to the fourth day and wrote down the sun did it "hit" her. She said she hurried to write down the fifth day before they thought to ask how the sun could have been created on the fourth day, but light on the first.

However, the sun, the moon, and the stars were already "there" when this account was written. Remember the time line; for the first time, these heavenly lights would have a religious significance for the Hebrews. Genesis describes this so clearly: "let them be for signs and for seasons and for days and years" (1:14). What a beautiful concept. Before this religious awareness developed, people worshiped the sun, the moon, and the stars. Now, for the first time, everything created was seen within God's might: The sun, the moon, and the stars would be used as God's religious time pieces. Sunset to sunset would define the time of worship for the Sabbath. Two of Israel's greatest festivals were celebrated at the beginning of the full moon: the Passover in the spring and the Feast of Booths in the fall. The sun and the moon marked religious celebrations. They were for rituals and ordinances.

On day five, all the fish of the sea and fowls of the air are created. When you talk about Genesis, people always ask why ticks and mosquitoes aren't mentioned in the creation account. This question, and its answer, is similar to the dinosaur issue. What is mentioned in Genesis is about creating the form and structure for everything that would later be used for religious awareness. In this context, ticks and mosquitoes do not have a religious significance. Every living thing mentioned in this creation story appears again in its intended use in the Book of Leviticus, in the formulas for sacrifice and offerings.

Then we have day six, the creation of the land animals and human beings. God is not creating a human person here, we already saw that. Human beings had long existed. But with Adam, God is creating the human capacity for spirituality. Remember that beautiful line from Genesis, "God formed man from the dust of the ground, and breathed into his nostrils the breath of life; and the man became a living being"(2:7).

The language in the beginning of the second chapter of Genesis is touching. Before Adam and Eve, there is no one to till the ground (2:5). The people on earth do not understand there is a God. With "Adam," there is a "living being" to accept the Covenant and begin working the fertile soil of faith. There is a mist coming up from the ground because God had not caused it to rain upon the earth. Could there be any more beautiful poetry? Until that point, humankind had tried to find God, but there was little understanding of the spiritual waters coming down from the heavens to water the earth. What light this casts on John's Gospel when he calls Jesus the life-giving water, the only means to quench the religious thirst on the earth. Day six establishes the foundations for a "working religion." Yet, it is incomplete without the Sabbath.

On day seven God rested, and humankind's religious needs are completed and blessed in the Sabbath. Everything is in place—the earth is filled with animals and trees and human beings, and the heavens are filled with God and the heavenly hosts of angels. These insights set the chosen people of God apart from the rest.

The following summary will perhaps paint a clearer picture of the comparison.

Scientific descriptions of the beginning of the world:	Biblical description of the days of creation:	Concept:
1. big bang	1. light	1. there is a living God
2. fire	2. heavens	2. God dwells in heaven
3. meteorite impacts	3. water, dry land, plants	3. separation of the "earthly" and the "spiritual"
4. chemical reaction	4. sun, moon, stars	4. God's timepiece/ religious calendar
5. energy	5. fish, fowl	5. formula for sacrifice and offerings
6. volcanic activity	6. land animals, humans	6. blessed by God, humans become living beings
7. cloud of dust	7. God rests	7. Covenant is established and sanctified in worship of God

God saw that everything was good. Genesis describes the beginning of humanity's ability to figure out its relationship with the *Lord God*. It is laid out in the Hebrew Scriptures, and for the Christian it is completed in Christ Jesus. The Bible reveals, to each generation seeking this truth, the final plan and meaning of our faith in God.

I remember once mentioning at a Bible study how the number three meant completion. Someone asked how they came up with that in the first place. Again, Genesis is the beginning. That's where the original meaning behind the numbers stem. You will see that every number used in the Bible stands for something. These same numbers are seen throughout the Bible. For example, the first seven numbers are given their symbolic meaning in the creation account.

In Genesis, the number "one" represents God is one, the recognition that there is but one, true, living God. "One," of course, means the first, God seen as the alpha, the beginning. It also means unity or oneness. On the other hand, "two" represents duplicity. In Genesis, on the second day, the creation of night and day brings the concept of good versus evil, or opposition. "Two" represents choice. "Three" represents completion. In Genesis, on day three, the three elements needed for the promise of continued life are brought together: water, dry land, and the fruit tree whose seed is in itself. I once looked up everything in the Bible that involved the number three, and it is incredible how, throughout Scripture, the number three always suggests completion and being finished. For example, Jonah spends three days and three nights in the belly of a whale until he learns his lesson. Peter was asked three times by Jesus if he loved him to make up for his three denials, etc. On day four, the sun, the moon, and the stars were created for signs and season, the stars specifically were used for navigation and direction. "Four" represents north, south, east, and west, encompassing the "religious world" of the Israelites. It is important to remember that when they talked about the world, they were always talking about the religious boundaries of their world, not the world as we know it. "Five" signifies the law, as in the five books of the Pentateuch. It is the suggested number of offerings for sacrifice in Leviticus. "Six" is incomplete, an unfinished number because it always represents part of a plan that will only be made complete in the seventh. "Seven," the perfect number, represents God's plan fulfilled. God is the alpha and the omega, the beginning and the end, perfection. Religious belief is no longer void and formless; it has structure and is made holy in the Sabbath.

Adam and Eve

We have seen how the first chapter of Genesis is a symbolic account of the seven days of creation. In the second chapter, we are told of how Adam and Eve were created. For the next few minutes, write down your recollection of the following.

1. How does God form Adam?

____

____

2. How is Eve created?

3. Briefly describe what happens in the Garden of Eden.

4. After they are sent out of the garden, Eve gives birth to two sons. Name the two sons and who is the older, and list their two occupations.

____

____

____

5. One brother kills the other. Describe who kills whom and why.

____

____

____

____

6. After the one brother kills the other, he is sent off to be a fugitive. What is he specifically afraid will happen to him?

____

____

____

____

7. Write down as much as you remember about this brother after he is banished from the land.

____

8. In the account of Genesis, Eve later gives birth to only one more child. Name the child.

Well, how much did you remember? The following is the basic storyline people shared with us. God formed Adam from the soil of the earth and then breathed life into him. After God caused Adam to fall into a deep sleep, God formed Eve from one of Adam's ribs. (Everyone remembered the rib.) Now Adam and Eve are both in the Garden of Eden, Paradise, and are told by God that they may eat the fruit of any tree in the garden except the tree that gives knowledge of good and evil. The serpent tricks Eve to take a bite of the apple. She gives it to Adam, and they immediately realize they are naked. (It's interesting that most people picture the fruit being an apple, but the Bible never mentions what kind of fruit it is.) Because they ate of the forbidden fruit, they are put out of the Garden of Eden, and from that time on Adam will have to work hard to till the ground, and Eve will now have pain in childbirth. (We all seem to remember that part.) Shortly after their banishment from the garden, Eve conceives a son whom she names Cain. She conceives a second time and names this son Abel.

Cain is the farmer, Abel the shepherd. Because of jealousy, Cain, the older brother, kills Abel. (Many people can never remember if Cain killed Abel or vice versa.) Abel's blood, spilled out on the ground, cries out to God. Cain, who was a tiller of the earth is now sent off to be a fugitive and a vagabond. For most of us, the story of Cain and Abel ends right at the point when Cain killed his brother. Did you remember what Cain is specifically afraid will happen to him once he is banished? Picture the scene. Cain must leave the land, and he is afraid that anyone who finds him will kill him. And so the Lord sets a mark upon Cain to protect him.

Take a few minutes to think about and answer the following questions.

1. **List the people who are mentioned in the creation account up until this point.**

2. **Considering the storyline thus far, who are the people Cain is afraid will kill him, and where did they come from?**

3. **Does this lead to any conclusions about the story of Adam and Eve?**

4. To further understand this point, draw a family tree using "the family" described in the creation story, beginning with the parents, Adam and Eve, and see how far you can get trying to establish the origins of the human race.

As soon as we described this scene to our ninth-graders, and they pictured Cain going out into a *populated* world, Terry exclaimed: "Wow, that proves it isn't a literal story, 'cause if it was, where did all the other people come from?"

Think about it. I don't think the story is trying to deceive us. It is obviously not the literal story of the first two people who "started" the human race. This is not an attempt to figure out our origin. As Ryan, a girl with great expression, put it: "When I was trying to picture it that way, there was only one other possibility." I can still see her raising her eyes to the ceiling, as she said: "And I don't even want to go there!"

Fundamental literalists sometimes use the argument that we can assume Adam and Eve had other children, sons and daughters who just weren't mentioned. In the written account, Eve gives birth to only one more child, another son named Seth. You can't have it both ways. If you take the Bible literally, you can't add pieces to the story to make it fit a point you're trying to make. The story makes perfect sense for the teaching the author intended.

It has always been common practice for religious traditions to use myth as a form of teaching to express the deeper truths that go beyond empirical limits of time and space. Yet, for some people it is difficult to accept the writing in Genesis as myth. For a long time, Catholics thought of the word "myth" as offensive, probably because we associate myth with fairy tales and things that "aren't true." I've even heard people say: "If the story of Adam and Eve didn't *really* happen, then everything else I've believed about the Bible isn't true either."

I'm almost embarrassed to admit that when I heard the Adam and Eve story as a child, I never even got as far as Ryan in my questioning. It amazes me when I think of it now. It is quite apparent that the story of Adam and Eve giving birth to three sons could not have had as its concern an explanation of how the earth was populated. On a deeper level of understanding, I've come to realize that the real concern was with the line of Hebrew inheritance. Again, a religious purpose. The inspired author was concerned with teaching the concepts of the origins of when humans first credited God with creating "the heavens and the earth."

The Fulfillment

The Hebrew Scriptures tell the story of Israel being the chosen people with whom God established the first Covenant. On the road to Emmaus, however, there were two Jews who began to see these Scriptures in a different light, as Jesus explained to them what was said about him in all the Scriptures, beginning with Moses and the writings of the prophets. Their eyes were opened to realize that what the prophets had written had now been fulfilled in the person of Jesus Christ. This small group of Jewish believers became the foundation for the Christian faith. We now live and share this faith in a community we call the one, holy, catholic, and apostolic Church.

For Christians, the Hebrew Scriptures and the New Testament are two inseparable books. We cannot begin to understand who Jesus is without understanding what Jesus came to fulfill. The Bible is one complete vision of the Christian religion from beginning to end. Through the inspiration of the Holy Spirit, every written word teaches and inspires beyond its literal meaning. We can never add to it, nor take away from it; and we will never exhaust its riches.

Fill in the blanks and compare.

The first Covenant:

______________________________.

1. The first three words of Genesis are

______________________________.

2. The world was in total

______________________________.

3. Then God created

______________________________.

The second Covenant:

______________________________.

1. The first three words of John's Gospel are

______________________________.

2. Can you guess what two things are mentioned in both Genesis and John's Gospel?

____

____

Genesis begins with the words, "In the beginning...." Listen to the beautiful language of this account. "In the beginning when God created the heavens and the earth, the earth was a formless void and darkness covered the face of the deep, while a wind from God swept over the face of the waters. Then God said, 'Let there be light'; and there was light"(1:1-3).

Now listen to the beginning of John's Gospel. "In the beginning was the Word, and the Word was with God, and the Word was God. He was in the beginning with God. All things came into being through him, and without him not one thing came into being. What has come into being in him was life, and the life was the light of all people. The light shines in the darkness, and the darkness did not overcome it" (1:1-5).

It is no coincidence that John chose to begin with the same three words as Genesis. They were written for a specific teaching purpose. Genesis uses the words, "In the beginning," to describe the event of a new and heightened religious awareness being created. John used the same three words to tell his readers that a similar event was happening all over again. In both accounts, three symbols are emphasized: beginning, darkness, and light. John intends this similarity to show that a new religious awareness has come about in Jesus Christ.

Following each word or phrase, write the most obvious match from what we've discussed.

Moses: ____

first Covenant: ______________________________________

"In the beginning": ___________________________________

Adam:____

sin: ____

paradise lost:__________________________________

In the New Testament, Paul refers to Jesus as the last Adam who takes away the sin of the world and restores paradise to humankind. The fulfillment becomes clear: the Hebrew Scriptures tell us that with Adam, sin was brought into the world, whereby paradise was lost, and the New Testament tells us thatwith Jesus Christ, the new Adam, who takes away the sin of the world, paradise is restored (1 Corinthians 15:22). In this very process, the end of the world happened. Now, that's a term wenever discussed when we were growing up.

This is another example of why it is so important to understand the language in the Bible. Many people are convinced, mistakenly, that the end of the world is coming. Fundamentalists point to passages in the Bible predicting a future cataclysmic event, but they fail to see that "the end of the world" has already taken place. As we have seen, "the world"—as used in the Bible—refers to the religious world and not the physical world. So, for those who believed that Jesus is the Messiah promised in the Hebrew Scriptures, the "end of the world" came to pass with the coming of God's reign in Christ. It was the end of a religious period of time, the "fullness of time." Jesus' death brought an end to the old "structure" of religion and a new beginning for anyone who accepted the teaching of Jesus.

This is the chart we did with our ninth-graders.

Moses	**Jesus**
first Covenant	**second Covenant**
"In the beginning"	**"In the beginning"**
Adam	**Jesus, the last Adam**
sin	**sin forgiven**
paradise lost	**paradise regained**

In sharing this concept with them, and explaining the biblical concept of the end of the world, we could actually see the visible relief spread across their faces.

Much of our work in the Church is to help prepare our young people, especially before they leave for college, to have a strong foundation of the faith, something that will not, later, fall apart.

When Things Make Sense

At the beginning of each session of this miniseries course, we always ask our kids to write down a question they have about God, religion, or the Bible, not because we think we have the answers, but because it doesn't make sense to "just teach" them and never let them ask the real questions they have—questions which are always profound in their own way.

One of the questions one boy asked fits in very well with what we've discussed. Please take a few minutes to write how you would have answered his question.

Why is the Bible called The Bible?

These are the fun questions that help us learn what our children are thinking. As we seek to explain them, they bring us all to a deeper level of the meaning of The Bible.

This is the way we explained it. Before the invention of paper or papyrus, the sacred writings were written down on leather scrolls. Papyrus was first imported from an ancient Phoenician city called *Byblos* (in present-day Lebanon). When the various writings of the Hebrew Scriptures were translated into Greek, they were also transcribed from scrolls to papyrus and gathered into one volume called "the holy books," that is, the Bible, meaning *"the book."* Think of the connotation of the word Bible. In our culture, we use the word to mean any book that is the definitive authority on a subject. For example, the best book on the subject of automobiles might be called the bible of automobiles, etc. But "The Bible" is the book of books, the authority on belief and religious practice. When we think it's authoritative on something else, e.g., science or history, that's when things get confused and no longer make sense.

As parents, we are a generation caught in the middle. Our parents did not read or study the Bible. Growing up, we weren't encouraged to do so either, and we simply did not have the scholarship available to us. I truly hurt for that person who said: "If Adam and Eve are not real, then everything else I've been taught about the Bible is a lie." It was like being taught your whole life that two and two is four and then suddenly someone saying, "Oh, by the way, two and two is really five." The whole foundation on which their faith was based suddenly collapsed. That's why adult religious education is so imperative at this particular time in the Church. How else are we to pass on the light of faith to our children?

One parent said she was really excited to finally get the symbolic meaning of the story, but it also left her confused about how to read the Bible stories to her two little ones. Reading the Bible stories to your children should be no different than reading any other story. You wouldn't begin by trying to teach your children the hidden symbolism contained in the story. Your responsibility as a parent is simply to read the beautiful stories to them until they know them by heart. As they get older, they'll begin to ask questions on their own, and that will be the time to explain the symbols and deeper meaning behind each story.

Faith is a journey. We cannot separate our questions from our own faith experience. That is the reason the *Keepers of the Light* has been written as a companion—if not a prerequisite—to this family Scripture series. Together, they put our questions of faith into perspective before we move on to the questions from a new generation.

In Conclusion

As we come to the end, I would like parents/teachers to answer the following three questions for yourselves.

1. How does this approach to the Genesis story affect you?

2. Were there any questions or concepts in the creation story that were left unanswered in your religious experience?

3. Have your children/students asked questions about creation that you were uncomfortable answering? Describe.

We have seen many unique answers to those three questions. Once you have answered them individually, discuss/share the general outcome with your spouse/other adults. I would like to end with one woman's very brave and moving statement.

She was a volunteer in the religious education program in our parish, teaching ages four and five. She had three children: a seven-year-old and two in high school. One afternoon, as she put it, both of her older children came home from school and ganged up on her over the scientific theories on evolution they were learning about in school. They asked her point blank: "Which is true, Mom, what we learn in science or what we read in the Bible?" She shrugged her shoulders and threw up her hands as she relayed her answer: "I told them not to believe a word their teachers said, that they didn't know what they were talking about." She laughed sheepishly, "What else could I say?"

What science teaches about evolution and what the Bible teaches about creation are not in opposition to each other. The Scriptures are not about that kind of story. Whenever we try to impose scientific questions on the Bible, we are not only missing the point, but doing a grave injustice to what the inspired authors intended to teach.